Playing Your First Music Festival

A Mini-Guide to Performing at Open-Air, Green-Field, Music Festivals

Andy Reynolds

Copyright © 2024 by Andy Reynolds

All rights reserved. No part of this book may be used or reproduced in any form whatsoever without written permission except in the case of brief quotations in critical articles or reviews.

For more information, or to book an event, contact :

andy.reynolds@livemusicbusiness.com

http://www.livemusicbusiness.com

Cover design by Andy Reynolds

First Edition: November 2024

Contents

Introduction

Congratulations on achieving a significant milestone in your musical career: your first festival show. Whether you've won a battle-of-the-bands competition, have been gigging so consistently that festival promoters finally took notice, or have success on streaming platforms, performing for the first time at a festival can be a career-boosting, unforgettable highlight – provided you don't mess it up!

I see music artists mess up when they come to perform festivals because they are not prepared for the unique way an open-air festival operates. And, because every festival I've ever worked at has a similar way of doing things, I can tell you what you need to do to lessen your chances of having a terrible show. I spend my summers visiting festivals around the world, working with the music artists booked at the huge, established events such as , , and , and some the smaller, or newly established like , or . The size of the festival is irrelevant; if you follow even some of the advice in this book, you will have a fantastic show.

Before we start, I'd like to clarify a few things.

First, this book is not about to how to get booked onto the bill of a music festival. I am assuming you have a confirmed slot at a festival and you are looking for advice on how to make the best of this opportunity (very sensible).

Second, I will use the term 'music artist' to describe you throughout this book. I used to say 'bands', and the days of the groups of musicians being the main format for music artists has long gone. I now use 'music artist' and that includes bands, solo performers, musicians, singers, and DJs.

Finally, this book describes the preparations for performing at 'green-field', or open-air, multi-stage festivals. I am usually referring to commercial festivals that have an audience capacity of 5000 people or more. The Music Festival Wizard (/) is a great resource that lists the type of festivals I am writing about.The three parts of this book

This book is in three parts.

- Part one, 'Advancing the Show', deals with the non-performance preparation of getting ready for a festival appearance.
- Part two, 'Rehearsing and Other Preparation', looks at how you can fine-tune your technical set-up, and perhaps even your music, to make the most impact when you get on stage
- Part three, 'On The Day,' guides you through what you should expect when you arrive at the festival site.

All green-field, open-air festivals are different, and yet they are all the same. There are conventions and practices to be observed; these conventions help countless music festivals go ahead without issues or challenges. A lot of what I am telling you in this book is about those conventions and practices. You might have different ideas about how you are going to approach your festival slot and, believe me, you won't get far if you don't observe the conventions.

Anyway, lecture over. Let's get stuck in.

Part One – Advancing the Show

Performing at a festival involves a lot more than turning up on the day. Festival organisers and promoters spend six to twelve months planning and organising their event. They need information from all the artists they invite to perform. In this part I will tell you what information they need, and what information you should ask from them. This exchange of information is called 'the advance'.

The 'Advance'

Festivals operate to strict timings - the conditions of the organiser being able to hold the festival in the first place rely on the fact that all 'noise' (glorious music to you and me) will finish at a certain time each day. Organisers must therefore get all the music artists they have invited to perform onto the stage and perform on time. Doing so means the other performers can also take the stage and that the festival will finish on time.

Festival organisers therefore draw up a schedule, or 'running order', for each stage. Multi-day festivals will have a running order for each stage, for each day. Performers are allocated a stage, an onstage time and a duration for their performance - forty minutes, for example. Performers are also allocated a period to set up their equipment prior to performance. We call this time period the 'changeover' time, a term you will read about a lot in this book. You can see an example of stage running orders in Figure 101.

The festival organisers will send the running orders to the performers. They will also send other information and a request for certain information from the performer. We call asking and supplying this information the 'advance' - the promoter 'advances' the show with the music artist, and vice versa.

You must engage with the advance process for each festival, well ahead of time. Read and understand the running order you are sent, if nothing else. You should make a note of your set time, set duration, and the start of the changeover period before your set.

Figure 101: A typical festival stage running order. This is from a stage at the Coachella Valley Music and Arts Festival, in California

The Changeover At A Music Festival.

The most important piece of information I can give you is this: you having a successful festival show depends on being ready for changeover time. I know we are going ahead of ourselves here (you've not even got in the practice room yet, let alone arrived at the festival to perform) and I cannot stress the importance of the changeover.

Music artists do not get a sound check for festival performances (unless they are headlining); the first time you set foot on the stage is during the changeover, immediately preceding your performance. Changeover times vary from festival to festival; you may have a thirty-minute changeover, you may have ten minutes. Figure 102 is an excerpt of a festival running order and indicates the changeover times as well as set times.

During changeover:

- The stage must be cleared of the previous music artist's people, crew, and equipment
- Your gear, people and crew members must get onto stage and get set up
- The monitor speakers, microphones, stage boxes and cables must be reset, plugged in, and tested.

That is a lot to accomplish in ten minutes.

Things can, and do, go wrong during changeover. Common issues include miscommunication about the artists's set-up, artist's equipment just not working, a musician leaving something in the dressing room and having to go back for it, or microphones being patched into the wrong channels. Unfortunately, the time taken to rectify such issues is deducted from the artist's performance duration. For example, a 40-minute set could be reduced to a mere 30 minutes if ten minutes is spent trying to fix an issue.

Like I say, changeovers can go badly. However, you can minimise the chance of things going wrong by making sure you understand about input lists, stage plans and rolling risers.

FRIDAY 17TH JULY 2015	
10:00	NOISE CURFEW LIFTED
12:00	GATES OPEN
23:00	STRICT NOISE CURFEW

MAIN STAGE		
21.30 - 22.45	75 mins	RUDIMENTAL
21.00 - 21.30	30 mins Changeover	Love Jones
20.00 - 21.00	60 mins	Cypress Hill
19.30 - 20.00	30 mins Changeover	Love Jones
18.30 - 19.30	60 mins	Mark Ronson DJ
18:20 - 18:30	10 mins Changeover	Love Jones
17:50 - 18:20	30 mins	Skepta
17:45 - 17:50	5 mins Changeover	Love Jones
16:45 - 17:45	60 mins	Rodigan
16:40 - 16:45	5 mins Changeover	Love Jones
16:10 - 16:40	30 mins	Ella Eyre
15:50 - 16:10	20 mins Changeover	Love Jones
15:00 - 15:50	50 mins	Blonde
14:40 - 15:00	20 mins Changeover	Love Jones
14:10 - 14:40	30 mins	Karen Harding
13:50 - 14:10	20 mins Changeover	Love Jones
13.30 - 13:50	20 mins	Ivy and Gold

STAGE 2 - WEST STAGE - THUMP		
21.00 - 22.30	90 mins	CATZ 'N DOGZ
	No Changeover	
19.30 - 21.00	90 mins	MK
	No Changeover	
18.30 - 19.30	60 mins	Shadow Child
	15 mins Changeover	
17.15-18.15	60 mins	Hercules & the Love Affair

SATURDAY 18TH JULY 2015	
10:00	NOISE CURFEW LIFTED
12:00	GATES OPEN
23:00	STRICT NOISE CURFEW

MAIN STAGE		
21.30 - 22.45	75 mins	SNOOP DOGG
21.00 - 21.30	30 mins Changeover	
20.00 - 21.00	60 mins	Hot Chip
19.30 - 20.00	30 mins Changeover	
14.50 - 15.10	20 mins Changeover	
13.40 - 14.50	70 mins	Craig Charles
13.30 - 13.40	10 mins changeover	
13.00 - 13.30	30 mins	Kiko Bun
	No Changeover	
12.30 - 13.00	30 mins	Icarus

This running order is given to the artists and their crew, and shows the set length and the changeover time alloted to each act.

STAGE 2 - WEST STAGE - NOISEY		
21.30 - 22.30	60 mins	LITTLE DRAGON
21.00 - 21.30	30 mins Changeover	
20.00 - 21.00	60 mins	Bonobo DJ Set
19.30 - 20.00	30 mins Changeover	
18.30 - 19.30	60 mins	Flight Facilities
18.05 - 18.30	25 mins Changeover	
17.20 - 18.05	45 mins	Danny Brown

Figure 102: The festival organiser will send you the set length and changeover time as part of the advance process.

The Input List & Stage Plan

A contributing factor to a successful changeover, and therefore a great festival gig, is to make sure the festival audio crew has an accurate and up-to-date input list and stage plan from you.

The promoter/organiser will ask you for your input list and stage plan as part of the advance process. They will also ask for other stage requirements, such as your rolling riser requirements (more on that in a bit) wireless in-ear monitor systems, backdrops, digital consoles, and pyrotechnics that you will need, or want to bring to the festival. The organiser will ask for this information by sending you a document to fill in. The document is usually an Excel or Google Sheets spreadsheet and many festivals now have online portals to gather the advance information. Whatever the format, you must reply and send them the requested information. Let's discuss your input list and stage plan.

The Input List

Your input list is a document that lists all the sound sources you need connecting into the public address (PA) sound system. See Figure 103 for an example*.

The input list is used by the festival audio crew to plan their work. They will be working with many artists on each of the festival, each with their own audio requirements. The input list you submit must be 100% accurate, and contain information relevant to their task on the day. I mentioned that changeovers can go badly; a common waste of time is the audio crew working from input lists that are out-of-date or that refer to non-festival performances.

Audio engineers have their own language and conventions. They are used to working from input list documents that are fit-for-purpose. Please do not try to create an input list if you don't know what you are doing. Instead, you should find an experienced live sound engineer (if you don't already work with one), and ask them to create it for you (see 'Spend Money On A Professional' later).

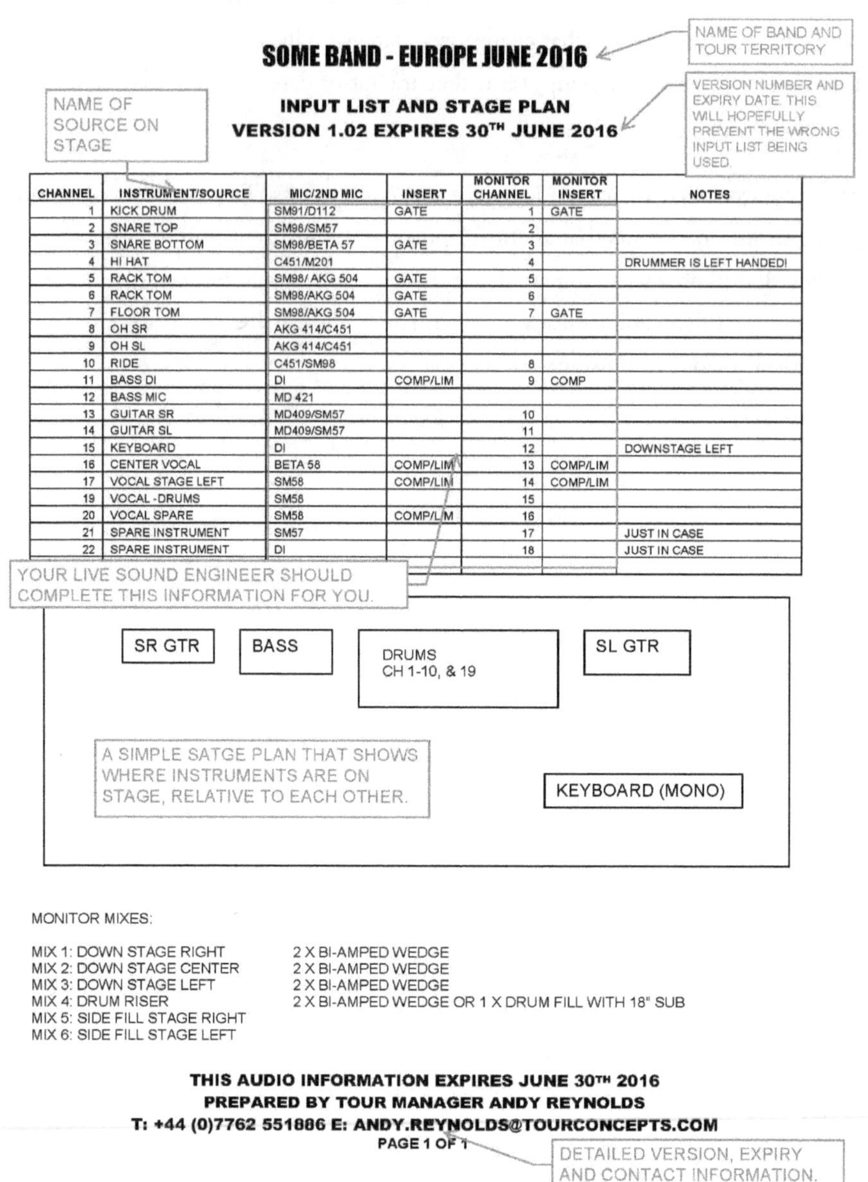

SOME BAND - EUROPE JUNE 2016

NAME OF BAND AND TOUR TERRITORY

INPUT LIST AND STAGE PLAN
VERSION 1.02 EXPIRES 30TH JUNE 2016

VERSION NUMBER AND EXPIRY DATE. THIS WILL HOPEFULLY PREVENT THE WRONG INPUT LIST BEING USED.

NAME OF SOURCE ON STAGE

CHANNEL	INSTRUMENT/SOURCE	MIC/2ND MIC	INSERT	MONITOR CHANNEL	MONITOR INSERT	NOTES
1	KICK DRUM	SM91/D112	GATE	1	GATE	
2	SNARE TOP	SM98/SM57		2		
3	SNARE BOTTOM	SM98/BETA 57	GATE	3		
4	HI HAT	C451/M201		4		DRUMMER IS LEFT HANDED!
5	RACK TOM	SM98/ AKG 504	GATE	5		
6	RACK TOM	SM98/AKG 504	GATE	6		
7	FLOOR TOM	SM98/AKG 504	GATE	7	GATE	
8	OH SR	AKG 414/C451				
9	OH SL	AKG 414/C451				
10	RIDE	C451/SM98		8		
11	BASS DI	DI	COMP/LIM	9	COMP	
12	BASS MIC	MD 421				
13	GUITAR SR	MD409/SM57		10		
14	GUITAR SL	MD409/SM57		11		
15	KEYBOARD	DI		12		DOWNSTAGE LEFT
16	CENTER VOCAL	BETA 58	COMP/LIM	13	COMP/LIM	
17	VOCAL STAGE LEFT	SM58	COMP/LIM	14	COMP/LIM	
19	VOCAL -DRUMS	SM58		15		
20	VOCAL SPARE	SM58	COMP/LIM	16		
21	SPARE INSTRUMENT	SM57		17		JUST IN CASE
22	SPARE INSTRUMENT	DI		18		JUST IN CASE

YOUR LIVE SOUND ENGINEER SHOULD COMPLETE THIS INFORMATION FOR YOU.

SR GTR

BASS

DRUMS
CH 1-10, & 19

SL GTR

A SIMPLE SATGE PLAN THAT SHOWS WHERE INSTRUMENTS ARE ON STAGE, RELATIVE TO EACH OTHER.

KEYBOARD (MONO)

MONITOR MIXES:

MIX 1: DOWN STAGE RIGHT 2 X BI-AMPED WEDGE
MIX 2: DOWN STAGE CENTER 2 X BI-AMPED WEDGE
MIX 3: DOWN STAGE LEFT 2 X BI-AMPED WEDGE
MIX 4: DRUM RISER 2 X BI-AMPED WEDGE OR 1 X DRUM FILL WITH 18" SUB
MIX 5: SIDE FILL STAGE RIGHT
MIX 6: SIDE FILL STAGE LEFT

THIS AUDIO INFORMATION EXPIRES JUNE 30TH 2016
PREPARED BY TOUR MANAGER ANDY REYNOLDS
T: +44 (0)7762 551886 E: ANDY.REYNOLDS@TOURCONCEPTS.COM
PAGE 1 OF 1

DETAILED VERSION, EXPIRY AND CONTACT INFORMATION.

Figure 103: An example input list & stage plan. A version number and expiry date are useful to avoid the wrong input list being used by a festival sound crew.

There is also a detailed explanation of input lists and how to create one on my YouTube channel at www.youtube.com/livemusicbusiness.

The Stage Plan

Figure 104 is the stage plan document of an international touring music act. The plan tells the festival audio crew what sound sources live in what positions on the stage for that act. Your stage plan does not have to be this detailed. It should simply indicate the relative position of your sound sources. At the very least, you should indicate the position of the sources, along with the channel numbers from your input list. You can always add notes to the stage plan if you think a particular part needs further explanation.

Labelling your input list and stage plan with expiry dates and version numbers is industry-standard practice. This labelling is similar to software version numbers. Every major change to your documents should be labelled with a new version number. The stage audio crew relies on your stage plan being correct and up to date. They use it to position your monitor wedges, power drops, and rolling risers on the day. Your equipment will be in the wrong place on stage if they are working off an out-of-date stage plan. You can see examples of version numbers and expiry dates in Figures 103 and 104.

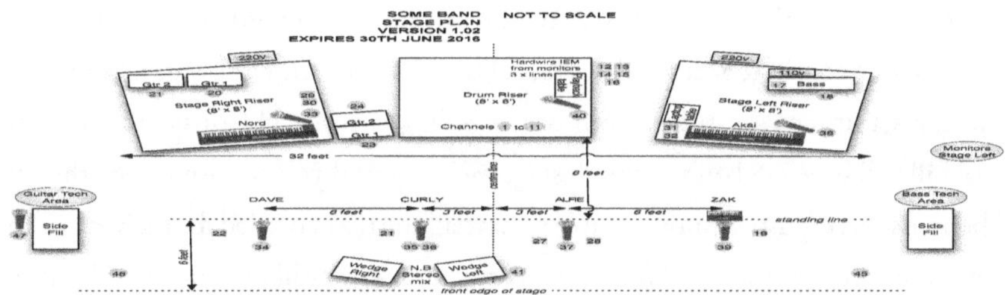

Figure 104: An example of a stage plan for an international touring act. Note the detailed explanations of which microphones go where, on-stage measurements, and even the names of the musicians performing. You do not need to provide this level of detail, however. A simple plan indicating relative position of your drum kit, amplifiers, keyboard set-up, laptop, etc;, will do.

The Rolling Risers

Rolling risers (Figure 105) are platforms on wheels which are used to help speed up changeovers. Your musical equipment is assembled on rolling risers, offstage, before the changeover. So, for instance, your drum kit will go on one riser, your keyboard rig will go on another, and so on. Guitar amps and stacks are placed on smaller platforms, called 'skids'. Using rolling risers enables each music act to have all their equipment set up, mic'd up, supplied with power, plugged into the PA system, and be made ready to push onto stage at the start of the changeover. This makes getting gear on and off stage quicker. The alternative is to carry each piece of musical equipment onto the stage and assemble it in place. This method wastes time and prevents technicians from testing and trouble-shooting before the changeover.

Festival organisers will ask you about your rolling riser requirements as part of the advance process, so make sure you specify what risers you need, and where they should end up on stage during the changeover. This information is a part of your stage plan.

Rolling risers are relatively big compared to the stage area. A riser for a drum kit will usually be 8' x 8' (2440mm x 2440mm). Two or more risers of these dimensions will take up a lot of room in the stage wings. A typical music act will need at least one riser (for the drum kit), and music acts that have lots of 'tech' (keyboard/electronics stations, extra percussion set ups, etc.) can need four or five rolling risers each. Consider that a typical festival bill will have 6-8 bands on each stage each day, and you can appreciate that space will be an issue. It is usually not possible to have all the risers needed for each act to be set up for the duration of the day. That would require something like twenty 8' x 8' platforms backstage - occupying an extraordinary amount of space. Because of the space constraints, we typically only use three or four sets of rolling risers, using them one after the other. A typical rolling riser sequence would be:

- Band A on stage on one set of risers.
- Band B, who are coming on next, gets their gear built on another set of risers. The band that has just finished performing (Band C) and is off stage, packing down their gear from a third set of risers.
- The stage crew then give the risers for Band C to Band D, who are on stage after

Band B.

This sequence helps keep backstage space requirements to a minimum. Only three sets of risers need to be in use at any given time - two backstage being prepared and re-prepped, and one set for the band performing (see Figure 106).

What this means for you is that you will not have access to your risers until they become available in the sequence. Your first question to the stage manager on arrival at the festival therefore should be, 'What time can we get our risers?' The stage manager will have worked out the sequence and timing of the riser allocation, and will tell you. She will probably say, 'You are getting 'X's' risers' (where X is the name of a music act further down the bill). So, when X finishes their performance, their risers will be wheeled to the wings and cleared of their equipment. You can then build your gear onto those same (empty) risers (see Figure 107 and Figure 108). A quick look at the running order will tell you what time in the day this will be. Look again at Figure 102. Ella Eyre's changeover is scheduled for 3:50 PM. The stage crew probably gave her the risers Karen Harding used before. Those risers would have been clear for use at about 14:50 (off stage at 14:40 and ten minutes to strip off all Karen's equipment). Ella Eyre and her crew would therefore have one hour to set up all their gear, have the microphones placed, cables plugged into the PA system, and power supplied to the risers.

Figure 105: An empty rolling riser.

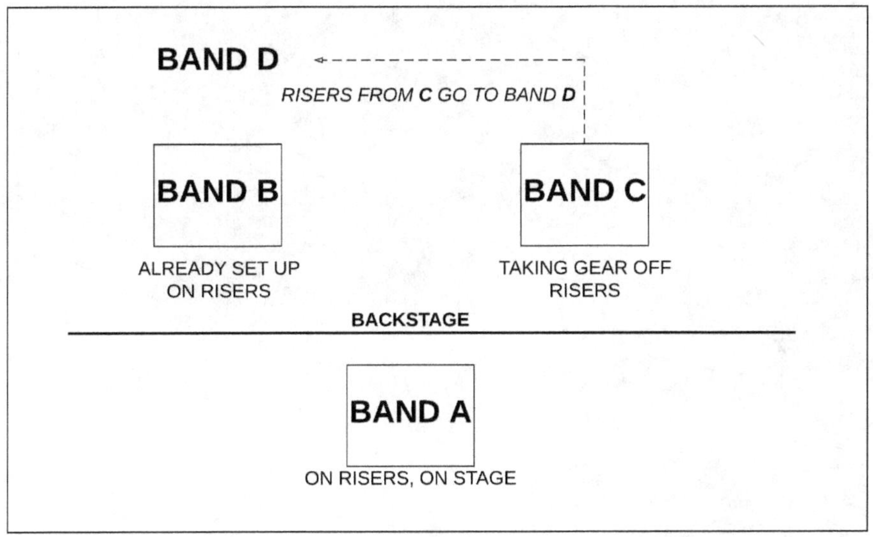

Figure 106: The sequence used for three sets of rolling risers at a festival.

Figure 107: Band equipment set up on a rolling riser, ready to go on stage at changeover time.

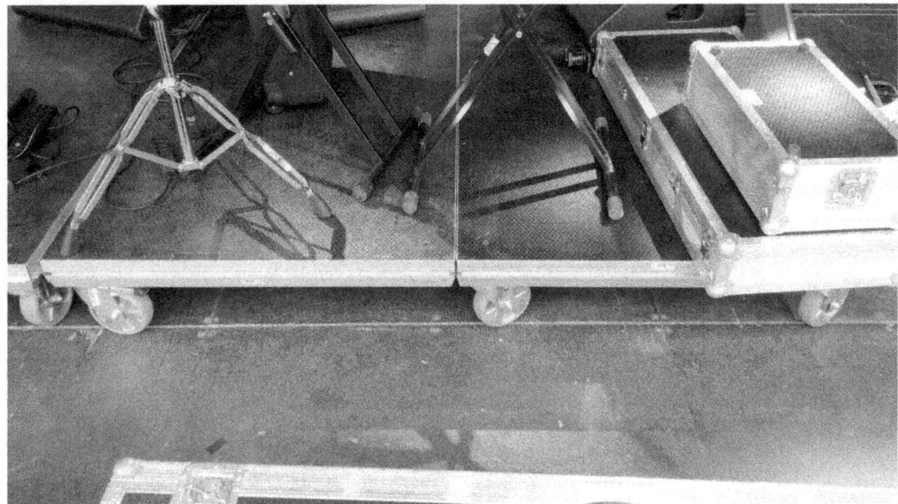

Figure 108: Another shot of risers, ready with band gear, waiting to be pushed forward at changeover.

Spend Money On A Professional

I don't mean to overwhelm you with all this talk of accurate stage plans, up-to-date input lists, and rolling riser allocations, but it's crucial for your musical career that your festival appearances go off without a hitch. People attend open-air, green-field festivals to experience fantastic music acts. There's fierce competition at each festival, and every music act has that one opportunity to captivate the crowd. If someone catches your performance while you're on fire, delivering a fantastic set and brimming with confidence, those individuals are likely to become your fans. You cannot afford to be ill-prepared or leave things to chance.

That's why I recommend investing in someone with extensive experience working with music acts at festivals. Open-air music festivals feature multiple music acts, quick changeovers, and less-than ideal operating conditions. Unfortunately, festivals are not the place for amateurs or inexperienced crew members.

To be clear, I advocate giving "new blood" a chance. Everything I do with my books, websites, and online courses, revolves around elevating the next generation of artists and crews to a professional level of success. However, if you want to make a powerful impression at your first festival, you must spend money and hire someone who knows the ropes.

Ideally, you need an experienced tour manager, a monitor engineer who understands your specific stage sound requirements, and a front-of-house (FOH) engineer who has mixed live audio on many open-air festival systems, often without a sound check. Considering that you probably can't afford to hire three separate individuals for your festival appearances, and since audio is the most critical aspect of organising your festival performance, I suggest you seek an experienced audio engineer and invest in their services. They will act as a go-between and translator between you and the stage audio crew, as well as mixing your live sound.

You don't have to hire a sound engineer exclusively, covering their transportation, accommodation, and other expenses for the concert. The person you need may already be on-site on the same day and be able to mix your sound as well. You can find an engineer in a number of ways. You could post in one of the many touring crew Facebook groups or on "roadie" job sites like Bobnet (), for instance (see Figure 109). Alternatively, you might know another music act on the bill—perhaps you've opened for them in the past—and may be familiar with their engineer. Your manager might also know the manager of another music act. Regardless of the scenario, there are ways to reach out and secure a talented, experienced engineer who can ease some of the stress associated with the advance process and deliver an outstanding performance on the day. Find out which engineers are already working at the festival for other music acts on the day of your performance, and see if they can assist you in mixing the sound and, more importantly, help you with the advance process (input lists, stage plans, riser requirements), and coordinate with the festival sound crew on the day.

And, since the audio engineer is already on-site and being paid by another music act, you should be able to negotiate a fee that serves as a bonus for them and is not too expensive for you. This is a common practice, with audio engineers, lighting designers, and backline technicians, working for two or more music acts during a festival (road crew often call this practice "double bubble" because they get paid twice).

Figure 109: Bobnet is one platform you should consider for posting a help-wanted advert seeking professional audio and lighting crew.

Put One Person In Charge

In the run-up to your first festival performance, there's a lot to think about beyond just your music. While your music is essential, you might overlook other aspects, such as the advance process, reviewing input lists, and arranging transport. Sometimes these tasks might be left too late or forgotten, which can jeopardise your show. It's crucial to organise everything well in advance and make sure it's completed. The best way to guarantee this is to have one dedicated person oversee it all.

I am a concert tour manager hired by bands throughout the year. My responsibilities, particularly the significance of the work, peak during the festival season. The vast amount of information demanded by festival organisers can be daunting. As a tour manager, I manage these organisational aspects for the music artists I represent. If you don't have a tour manager, assign someone you trust within your group or circle to act as the 'festival production manager'. This individual should manage the advance process, produce professional input lists, stage plans, catering riders, and fulfil any other requirements set by the festival organiser. Otherwise, crucial tasks might be missed unless someone focuses solely on them.

You might think your manager can handle this, but from my experience, it's not advisable. The workload for festival advancing is immense, and this could detract them from their primary responsibilities. It's more effective if your sound engineer, a band member, a reliable friend takes this role up, or even yourself.

Don't Assume Anything

Reading this, you might think, 'This doesn't concern me; I send out a contract rider specifying what I need for each show.' For typical gigs - such as clubs, bars, and theatres - you'd be correct. However, festivals and their organisers work under less than ideal conditions. They often can't fulfil the usual technical, stage, and hospitality requests you'd expect from a purpose-built music venue. Open-air festivals are erected just for the event and then dismantled afterwards. While organisers strive to ensure the comfort and safety of artists, crew, and the audience, there are limitations to what's feasible and affordable. As for your rider's demands, don't count on them. You might make any request, but they'll likely return your contract rider, marked with many clauses crossed out, accompanied by notes like 'festival conditions apply' or 'standard festival rider' (see Figure 110). So, never assume. The golden rule for festivals is simple: if you need something for your performance, bring it. Don't expect the promoter to provide it.

8. NA

CATERING & RIDER

11. The Promoter agrees provide at their own expense 2 x Full meals prior to performance to be served at the discretion of the Artist. Where a meal is not possible a £20 buyout per person per day must be made available. Hotel must have prepaid Internet access, or the promoter must pay for access.

The Promoter agrees provide at their own expense, the following refreshments to be placed in the dressing room no later than TWO (2) hours prior to performance:

- 10 x Premium Lager
- 2 x Large bottles of water
- Selection of healthy snacks (fruit, nuts, pretzels, chips, etc)
- 4 x bottles of orange juice
- Assorted soft drinks

TECHNICAL RIDER

STANDARD FESTIVAL RIDER

12.

(a) PA: The Promoter agrees to provide and pay for a first class PA system for this engagement at no cost to the Artist. All necessary crew and operators are to be in attendance throughout the entire duration of the Artist's performance. The PA should have powerful bass and produce 10-12 watts per person and should be adequate to the size and capacity of the club or festival.

(b) LIGHTING: A professional lighting system adequate to the size and style of the venue and stage is required. The DJ booth needs to be equipped with appropriate work light both near the DJ setup and in the area where artist equipment is placed.

(c) AUDIO ENGINEERING: A professional sound engineer who is either in-house at the venue or fully versed in the sound system for the event will be present during sound check and throughout the duration of the Artist's set. Artist requests access to the remote mixing console before and during the performance.

(d) MONITORING: 2 x monitors, with suitable amplification, are to be provided at Artists' ear level and must be

Figure 110: A contract rider that the promoter has amended to show that standard festival conditions and rider are in effect.

Part Two– Rehearsing and Other Preparation

You've filled in the form from the festival promoter asking about input lists, rolling risers and stage plans. Now it is time to think about how you will approach the show itself. The first step is to practice.

Practice Your Stage Craft

Clearly, you'll rehearse your music for your festival performance. However, it's also worth rehearsing other elements of your show.

For example, do you plan to use intro or walk-on music? I'd advise against it – it's tricky to synchronise and can seem over-the-top for a daytime festival slot. Do you need to switch guitars for different tunings during your set? If so, practise this change in advance and time how long it takes. Festivals enforce strict running orders and timings. Overstepping your slot because you took three minutes (equivalent to half a song) to change guitars is a no-go.

Another aspect worth rehearsing is your stage entrance – and I'm not talking about perfecting a rock-star strut. It's about the sequence in which you appear. Getting this wrong can diminish a band's impact. For instance, if your opening track begins with a drum solo, consider having the drummer enter first, establish the beat, and then have the rest of the band follow. Otherwise, everyone coming on stage, adjusting their instruments, and then waiting for the drummer can look disjointed and amateur. This delay might cause some audience members to leave before you've played a single note. Which leads me to...

The Audience Is Not There to See You (Or Anyone Else).

Open-air music festivals used to focus on a particular type or style of music. The , which inspired , was primarily a rock festival, often hosting prominent US rock bands. in Belgium consistently featured alternative and progressive rock bands, targeting a progressive younger audience. ('Pukkel' translates to 'pimple', indicating their primary audience: teenagers.) In the past, if a festival booked you, it was because your style matched the festival's genre.

However, festival line-ups have developed, mirroring the way we discover music in this digital age. Jay Marciano, the head of , a festival promoter, says, "Festivals reflect how fans are consuming music in a digital world. It's sampling[1]". This shift means the typical summer festival now showcases a diverse blend of genres and styles. The audience doesn't align with a specific musical taste; they're there to explore various acts and hope to be entertained. This principle of audience sampling applies to almost all acts, perhaps except for the headliners. While capturing the attention of these casual 'samplers' is essential to being successful (and clearly you are good, given you've been invited to perform), remember that most attendees aren't there specifically for you. Thus, every band, including yours, has an equal opportunity to win over new fans.

Figure 201: Reading Festival in England. The inspiration behind the original travelling Lolapalooza festival, and a showcase of alternative rock music.

Plan Your Set List...And Be Ready To Adapt.

Planning a festival set list is a balancing act. You need to impress an audience with songs they might not know, all in a setting that might not be perfect. (Many open-air festival stages have sound restrictions, so your music might not sound as powerful as you'd like to the crowd). You want variety in your set, but you don't want the energy to dip so much that people get distracted and wander off.

If you're a lesser-known act, it's crucial to captivate your audience early on. So, feature at least two of your best tracks within the first four songs of your set.

Much of this mirrors advice I've given before. However, festivals come with unique challenges compared to indoor gigs. Unexpected weather shifts, rowdy attendees, power outages, and other unpredictable events can all divert attention from your performance. While it's essential to have a planned set (for timing, among other reasons), it's also crucial to be aware of potential distractions and to be prepared to adjust accordingly. At the very least, have a contingency plan for technical hitches. My advice? If there's a tech issue, announce it and exit the stage until it's resolved.

Tent Or Open Air

A factor that will determine your set list, and the material that goes in it, is whether you will play on an open-air stage or inside a tent. It is easier to recreate a club or a small theatre environment in a tent, and so you may choose a more intimate set, or slower songs if your stage is a tent.

Should You Perform Cover Versions?

No.

You might know my stance on performing cover versions: why use your valuable public exposure time to showcase someone else's work? However, a quick Google search for performing hints and tips for musicians at festivals returns results that show I am in the minority. I firmly believe that you'd want an audience to connect with you and your original music, rather than a rendition of someone else's track. Unless it's been raining all day, and then the sun comes out. In which case, you better have had rehearsed a version of 'In The Summertime'...

Talking Between Songs

I'm often surprised to see talented stage performers approach an open microphone during a performance break and spout absolute nonsense. Or when a lead singer delivers a heartfelt speech, only to be interrupted by the drummer and bass player starting the next song, completely overshadowing her.

Speaking is as much a part of the performance as the music. Just because you're a skilled musician doesn't automatically make you a confident and eloquent public speaker. Nor does it mean your bandmates are aware you'll deliver a planned speech.

From my experience, I suggest keeping the banter between songs brief and somewhat rehearsed. Avoid mumbling, but don't shout either. Ensure you introduce your band at least twice during the set (as highlighted in 'Tell The Audience Who You Are'). Refrain from talking or shouting over the beginnings or ends of songs. When rehearsing, designate moments between or during tracks for the vocalist to speak or make announcements.

How to Deal With Hecklers

Do not respond to hecklers. Try not to feel upset or enraged by their comments. You are onstage and you are entertaining. Arguments with members of the audience take away the focus from you and alienate other members of the audience. Concentrate on wowing the masses and not on arguing with individuals.

Appreciate the Sound Level Limits

A contemporary open-air, green-field music festival can be a colossal event, taking weeks to set up and dismantle. This results in a significant impact on the nearby area due to increased traffic, people, waste, and noise. It's only appropriate that local authorities request festival organisers to minimise the event's effects on the surroundings. The need to decrease 'noise' (which we see as beautiful music) means that these authorities often impose strict sound pressure level constraints to prevent 'noise breakout', which can disturb both human and wildlife inhabitants near the venue.

I bring this up because a sound pressure level restriction on the stage where you'll be performing will be communicated to you (refer to figure 202). This restriction will challenge your Front of House (FOH) engineer in delivering a powerful and clear mix. The combination of sound level constraints, along with potential wind and rain, can conceal many subtleties in your music. Please resist the urge to "game the system." Gone are the days of using tricks like sticking chewing gum on microphone ends to fool sound measurements. Festivals now ensure artists stick to the set levels and often employ specialised noise measurement consultants for this task. Often called 'the noise police', these people are diligent and have encountered every trick used to bypass the sound pressure limits. Therefore, accept that you cannot override these limits. Support your FOH engineer by reducing your backline amp volumes, positioning your drum kit as far upstage as workable, and maintaining a low wedge volume (or using in-ear monitors if you have a dedicated monitor engineer). It's advisable to plan your approach to a quieter stage during rehearsals before your performance.

NOISE MANAGEMENT

Lost Village festival engages the services of Three Spires Acoustics to assist with the environmental impact of noise generated by the festival. We are keen to be responsible to our neighbouring residents, businesses and schools and ensure that our impact on them is minimal.

Three Spires Acoustics have undertaken noise modelling of the site and noise sources to provide recommended noise levels that ensure compliance with the conditions set out in the premises license. These recommended noise levels must be adhered to by all stages.

Three Spires Acoustics will be onsite working in direct correspondence with the Production Manager and the festivals PA operators instructing any required adjustments to ensure noise conditions are met. We expect that all guest engineers and production teams work with us and Three Spires Acoustics to ensure the festival fulfils its licensing obligations.

The curfew time of the stage is set to comply with the festivals licence conditions and cannot be broken. There cannot be any extension to set times under any circumstances in order to comply with the event curfew.

There can be no use of festival PA systems before the hours of 09:00am under any circumstances. This means that all sound check requests must fall outside of this curfew and within the stage opening times.

If there are any questions or further information required regarding noise management, please contact the Production Manager.

LOST VILLAGE 2018 PRODUCTION INFORMATION

Figure 202: Extract from a festival 'artist information' document explaining the sound volume limits in place.

Make Your Audio Festival Friendly

While audiences attend to 'see' a band perform, it's actually the audio they react to most. They'll be tuning into the beats, notes, textures, and the overall volume of your music.

In a perfect setting, like your own club gig, you'd have the luxury of setting up your equipment on stage, testing it out, attaching microphones and DI boxes to every sound source, linking them to the sound system, and then conducting a thorough sound check. This ensures the FOH engineer achieves the right levels and EQ, and that you have an optimal sound experience on stage, either through monitor wedges or in-ear monitors. If you've been around, you'd know this process can sometimes span up to two hours, contingent on your acts' intricacies. If you've gone through Part One - 'The Change Over', you'd also be aware that many open-air, green-field festivals don't offer the privilege of sound checks. You might find yourself with a mere 10 minutes to set everything up on stage, connect it to the audio system, and get going.

The hasty prep to get stage-ready and ensure crisp audio through the PA isn't the best scenario. This compressed setup time, filled with rushed actions, heightens the risk of things taking a wrong turn. It's wise, then, to keep your musical set-up streamlined. Given the nature of festival stages, there's not much scope for intricate details. So, it's best to eliminate anything in your arrangement that might get 'lost' in the sound or pose issues during transitions and performances.

Another compelling reason for a streamlined setup is the potential unfamiliarity of the monitor engineer with your music. Unless you bring along your personal monitor engineer, the festival's appointed engineer – who might not know your music, equipment, or even you until the changeover – will handle your stage audio. By simplifying the instruments on stage, the number of inputs into the audio system is reduced, which allows the monitor engineer to easily create mixes for each musician.

Bearing this in mind, here are my suggestions for festival-friendly equipment adjustments you might want to consider:

Make It Mono

You do not need your keyboards to be in stereo (have both left and right outputs connected to the audio system). You do not need a stereo guitar set up with two guitar amp/cabs. Reduced sound levels (see 'Sound Volume Limits'), and atmospheric conditions at festivals (wind, rain, etc) make subtleties such as stereo chorus effects redundant. Consider this - every second output from keyboards, drum machines, etc., you strip out of your set-up will half your channel count. Which should mean less time to get your backline patched into the sound system.

Use One Guitar or Bass for the Whole Set

Your '56 Telemaster Moonshine re-issue might sound perfect for that song midway through your set, but switching guitars takes time. Considering how cold and windy festival stages can be, you'll also need to check if it's still in tune. With likely just a 20-minute slot, every second counts. Swapping fewer instruments might let you squeeze in an extra song. I get that transitioning from an electric to an acoustic once might be necessary. However, I'd advise against band members switching instruments multiple times during a short set. Sure, big bands seem to change guitars for every song, but they've got dedicated guitar techs on standby. So, until you've climbed higher up the festival ladder and have your own guitar tech, stick to one main guitar for your set. Always keep a spare guitar handy though – you never know when you'll snap a string or have a strap issue!

Don't Use Vocal Effects 'In-Line'

Vocal effects units, such as the Boss VE20 (see figure 203), are common. People use them 'in-line', meaning the vocal mic plugs directly into the unit. These units can apply effects, often that popular harmonising/pitch-shift feature prevalent in many songs today, to the vocal. The blend of the original vocal signal and the effects emerge from the unit as a mono output. However, my experience with these units in a live setting hasn't been great. The vocal might sound acceptable when the effect is in bypass mode, but it can produce overwhelming feedback when the effect activates. There are straightforward audio reasons for this. As this isn't a technical guide, we'll leave the detailed explanation for another time. What you need to know is that introducing the effect to the vocal signal chain, especially when the vocal dominates the stage monitor wedges, can lead to audio 'coupling', which might induce feedback. Adjusting the inputs and outputs on the effects units can prevent this signal path mismatch, but it's challenging during a 20-minute festival changeover.

Another concern is that these units often rely on batteries (which might be drained if you forget to switch off the unit post-show) or mains power — that's if you remembered to bring the correct power supply unit (PSU). Connecting your device to the mains demands a power 'drop' downstage. You did request that power drop downstage before the changeover, right? If not, the stage crew will need to set one up for you, all while managing other mics, DI boxes, and testing. It might appear minor, but I've witnessed several festival changeovers go awry because of a faulty vocal effects box or the absence of the right power supply for the unit.

Figure 203: A typical in-line vocal effects unit, the Boss VE20. Please do not use this 'in-line' on a festival stage.

No Microphones for Shakers and Other Quiet Percussion

Keyboard players, backing singers, and other performers who aren't busy with both hands often receive percussion instruments such as shakers, cabasas, afuche, or 'eggs' (see Figure 204) to play during the set. However, the audio level these items produce is quite soft compared to a voice or guitar amp, so we often assign a microphone specifically for these shakers. But during the rush of creating a mix in a festival setting, the person mixing FOH audio might forget to amplify the shaker mic or struggle to achieve a sufficient level for the shaker to stand out amongst the other instruments on stage. What's the outcome? It often proves a futile effort. Setting up a microphone for the shakers requires the audio crew to introduce another mic, on another stand, and connect it as an additional input, which they must also test during the changeover. This process consumes more precious time and often yields minimal impact during the actual performance. Shakers and cabasas excel in the studio. Stick to using them there, or at the very least, avoid trying to amplify them for a festival gig.

Figure 204: Percussion eggs - great in the studio. Please leave them there.(Picture courtesy of Lone Star Percussion)

In-ear Monitors? Have Your Own Engineer

You may have your own in-ear monitor pack and moulds, and you will know the fantastic level of detail and clarity you can get when your in-ear mix is set up correctly. So read that last part again, and imagine what your in-ear mix will sound like if a person who has never met you, or heard your music before, is trying to set up a mix for you and everyone else on stage, in 20 or fewer minutes. In-ear audio is unforgiving. So again, perhaps keep it simple and stay on monitor wedges for your festival performance, or hire a dedicated monitor engineer who knows how to set up your monitor mix.

Don't Ask for Delay or Reverb In Your Wedge Monitors

You should think about simplifying another aspect of your on-stage monitor mix: the use of effects on your vocals. I'm not talking about effects from effects boxes as discussed earlier, but those the engineer applies from their console. Using audio effects in wedges can lead to the 'coupling' phenomenon I discussed earlier, resulting in feedback. Even the most seasoned monitor engineer might struggle to balance the right amount of reverb in your wedges without causing feedback. Reverb also makes sounds seem 'distant' and faded. If you want a clear and loud vocal in your wedges, why introduce an effect that makes your voice sound subdued and far away?

Don't Ask for Effects or Volume Cues

Consider a request like this: 'I need a big reverb swell on the last line of the third verse, and again on the outro of the second section of the song with the shakers.' Hmmm.

Don't expect strangers who haven't met you or are unfamiliar with your music to deliver specific audio (or lighting) effects on cue. For context, music acts that coordinate audio and visual effects cues often spend days, if not weeks, in pre-production rehearsals, fine-tuning these timings. You and the on-stage audio team won't have this luxury during a festival change-over. Thus, it's both unrealistic and naïve to assume a festival audio professional can accurately execute your effect requests on the spot.

Make Every Instrument Count

While in rehearsal, examine your set-up and evaluate which instruments you use for each song. Do you have an instrument or sound source that needs its own mic or DI, but is only used in one song? Perhaps a quirky vintage drum machine for a song's intro? Or the melodica (see Figure 205) showcased in the chorus of your hit? Are these sounds essential for your festival show? Can other instruments you frequently use mimic them? My goal is to help you minimise the number of instruments, microphones, and DI boxes you need on stage (refer to 'Make It Mono' above). Reducing complexity can lead to a smoother change-over and a more relaxed performance.

Figure 205: A person playing a melodica. Do you have to use it for your festival show?

Dont Use Vintage Instruments

Old gear might look and sound impressive, but audio equipment from the 60s, 70s, 80s, and 90s isn't reliable. Transporting them, varying climates, and voltage changes can all negatively affect this old equipment. Remember, a festival stage differs from a studio. The unique nuances of that retro sound might get lost through a festival system, especially if sound volume limits apply (refer to 'Appreciate the Sound Level Limits'). Instead of relying on vintage gear, consider software plug-ins or re-issued equipment to replicate your desired sound. This way, you'll avoid the stress of equipment failure during crucial moments.

You might see me as a 'kill joy' after going through my suggestions, but my aim is to enhance your festival experience. I genuinely want the best for you.

Appreciate the Use of Show Files

Modern live mixing consoles allow you to store and retrieve all settings. We refer to this saved data as a 'show file'. For example, a user can load a show file created on a Yamaha CL5 at one venue onto another CL5 at a different festival (Figure 206). This ensures that all the input gains, output fader levels, EQ adjustments, and effects are replicated on the second console. As a result, touring sound engineers save their show settings on a USB drive after each show. This means they don't need to bring their console on tour. Instead, they can arrive at the next venue, plug in the show file, and restore the settings from the previous show. This practice is also common for open-air music festivals. At the beginning of a band's changeover time, the FOH engineer provides her show file on a USB to the PA system's audio team, who then loads it onto the desk. While the process might seem straightforward, the reality is a bit more intricate.

In a standard venue where there's ample time for sound checks and tests, loading show files is straightforward. But in a festival setting, it's trickier. Many PA companies at festivals prefer to receive show files in advance when workable. This allows them to check the file's integrity, ensuring it loads properly, remains uncorrupted, is virus free, and that its inputs and outputs match the specific show requirements.

Show files can significantly expedite the process and ensure a consistent sound for both FOH and monitors. It therefore makes sense that you can supply a show file for your festival performance.

For your festival shows, determine the FOH and monitor console's make and model during the advance process. Then, send your engineer's relevant show file to the festival. If you don't have a dedicated monitor engineer, you can send monitor mix show files for each festival on your tour. This provides the festival's monitor engineer with a solid starting point for your on-stage sound, which you can adjust using hand gestures to show volume changes. There are several live mixing console models, and show files aren't universally compatible across manufacturers. Therefore, you'll need to craft a show file for each major pro-audio console brand, including:

- Yamaha
- DiGiCo
- Avid
- Soundcraft
- SSL
- Midas
- Allen & Heath

Note that some models may not even be compatible with their own brands!

To prepare show files for every situation, you'll need to hire the console, stage box, necessary cables, a spacious rehearsal room, wedges, amps, and all mics and DIs required for your full show back line. Set everything up in the rehearsal room with the console, rehearse your festival set, and adjust the monitor mix settings for each musician until everyone is content. Remember to save the settings on the console and create multiple backup copies of the show file. Since unforeseen issues can arise, having backups is crucial. And this process only covers one console brand. You'll need to repeat this for each of the six listed brands. Given the cost and time involved, hiring a professional monitor engineer for the festival season might be more economical.

Figure 206: A typical digital live mixing console - in this case the Yamaha CL5, which can be used for both monitor and FOH mixing.

Use Your Guest Tickets Wisely

One of the common challenges of being booked for a summer festival is the inevitable request from friends, family, neighbours, and parents for tickets. I've discussed this previously, and the same advice holds for festivals. Instead of using guest passes provided by the festival (if they offer any) for personal acquaintances, consider offering them to influential journalists from outlets like Pitchfork or Consequence. This way, they can enjoy the perks like clean backstage toilets, and in gratitude, they might write a positive review about your performance and your new album. While this approach might not sit well with your friends and family, remember, it's your music career. And when I mention the potential tickets you might receive, understand that getting guest tickets isn't a given (refer to Figure 207). Promoters likely won't hand out 10 tickets for every band performing when festival tickets cost $250.00 for the weekend or $80 for a day, right? So, if you secure festival guest tickets, allocate them strategically.

GUEST LIST

You are allocated one free weekend pass for someone to join you.
Please pass on their full name to us by the deadline below for confirmation.

co.uk

All guests must have ID and collect their passes from the Main Box Office.
Deadline for submission is FRIDAY 29TH JUNE

CONTACT

Figure 207: Festivals will try to reduce the number of guest tickets they allocate to you, for the obvious reason they are losing a lot of money on each free ticket.

Guests as Extra Crew - Don't Do It

A common tactic to bring additional people into a festival without guest list tickets involves listing them on the 'cast & crew' roster submitted to festival organisers. Promoters request this 'cast and crew' list of stage performers and crew during the advance process (refer to Part 1) to distribute the number of passes and to ensure that the total attendance doesn't surpass the limit set by licensing agreements.

Many music acts (and their managers) are tempted to add fake names to the crew list, using titles like 'hair & make-up' or inventing backline technician roles, which lets them bring extra friends and family in for free. While I've used this tactic in the past, I can attest it's neither wise nor professional, and you shouldn't depend on it or suggest it to those close to you. By inflating your cast and crew count, you increase costs for the promoters (extra pass printing, additional catering, etc.), expenses that get passed on to ticket buyers. This is one reason ticket prices can be high.

Another reason is that guests listed as crew can access dressing rooms, catering, and performance areas just like genuine band members and staff. It's concerning when a friend, whom you've disguised as a 'bass tech', drinks the booze meant for the band and behaves recklessly. Consider the complications if this friend damages property or disrupts the headline act's performance – scenarios I've witnessed with disguised "guests." Honestly, the risks outweigh the benefits. You have plenty to manage with your performance and the accompanying logistics, without the added stress of ensuring your friends behave responsibly.

Book Your Transport and Hotels Straight Away

The Pollstar 'Major Euro Music Festival Calendar - ILMC Bonus Edition[2]' reveals 213 festivals in mainland UK from May to September. That's a significant number of festivals in just the UK, hosting countless bands. Each of those bands will need transportation for both personnel and equipment. So, if you're considering hiring transport for your festival slot, book it as soon as you receive a tentative offer for the next year.

In the UK, mainland Europe, and now the USA, the most recommended vehicle is the splitter van (see Figure 208). These specialised touring vehicles can carry up to 9 people, including the driver, and store all your gear in a separate section. Gone are the days of sitting on top of your amps in a cargo van, which, besides being uncomfortable, breaks the law and compromises safety. You also have the option in the US for a 15-seat passenger van—removing seats post-rental—or attach a trailer to your rental.

If you own a van or car, ensure it's in reliable condition and has the required tax and breakdown cover before heading to the festival. Keep in mind that festivals might not have the best road conditions and your car or van might need to travel over rough ground.

Ensure you book your transportation once you receive a festival offer, regardless of your budget constraints. you can always cancel the vehicle reservation if the promoter doesn't confirm the event.

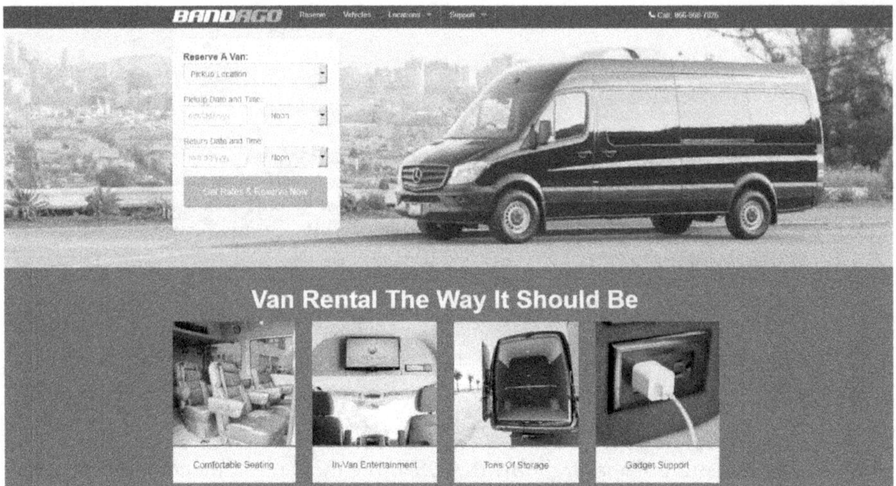

Figure 208: Splitter vans can seat up to nine people and have a separate space for musical equipment.

---

1. . Neil Shah, 'Music Festivals: Peace, Love and a Business Battle', Wall Street Journal, 30 July 2015
2. . 'Major Euro Music Festival Calendar ILMC Bonus Issue', Pollstar, 29 February 2016

Part Three – On The Day

You have taken care of all the show advancing, practised and prepared your set and everything else that goes into a performance, now it's time to pack up your gear, load out of the rehearsal room and head off to the festival itself.

Get There On Time

One of the many things that might irritate you after playing at festivals for a couple of years is the requirement to have your performing personnel and their equipment on site at least three hours before your changeover time. (Refer to part one for a reminder about changeover time).

When you perform at a bar, club, or theatre, you arrive early for a sound check. However, since you don't get the opportunity for a sound check at an open-air festival, it might seem odd to arrive at the gig so early. This timing can sometimes feel unnecessary, especially if the promoter hasn't invested in extra sets of risers, and you can only access yours 45 minutes before your changeover. But that's the way it is.

As it is, I support the three-hour 'rule'. Festival organisers introduced it because of bands consistently arriving late or not showing up, resulting in missed slots. So, it's right and professional to plan on being there three hours before your changeover.

Yet, arriving three hours early can be a hassle. For instance, if you're the first act on a particular stage, you might need to be on site extremely early. Most open-air summer festivals aim to provide a full day of live music, starting the first bands around midday. If they schedule you as the opening act at midday, you'll need to be on site by 09:00 am! Plus, if the festival site is far from your hometown and it's the first day of a multi-day event, expect heavy traffic. That means an even earlier start, which some of your band members might struggle with. Figures 301, 302, and 303 present excerpts from festival 'artist information' documents, highlighting the necessity for artists to arrive at least three hours before their stage time.

STAGE SET TIMES: The festival determines which stage and when the bands play in advance. It is vital that everyone keeps their performances within their allocated set times. Please keep checking the website for the latest times as they will change in the lead up to the festival.

ARRIVAL: You should plan to have all your equipment on site around 3 hours prior to your performance time.

SOUND & LIGHTING: Please see the specs in the Technical Document. If you do not have sound engineers with you, never fear there will be engineers to operate.

SOUNDCHECKS: Soundchecks will NOT be possible. Line checks will occur in the set change before your performance. When you use more than the appointed time for the change over, we will deduct this time from the set length. All show times include encores.

NOISE AND CURFEWS: The noise curfew is only lifted when the first band begins at 12 noon so there are no opportunities for soundchecks (no not even just monitors) before this. Official site opening house are 12 midday till 11pm on the Friday and 12 midday till 11pm on the Saturday.

POWER SUPPLIES: There will be 240v power drops across the stage. If you are bringing 110v equipment, you will need to bring transformers or arrange these with us. 110v transformers are an Artist cost unless provided by the Audio Company.

ROLLING RISERS: There will be rolling risers on the Main Stage (sizes 8' x 8' x either 1' or 2' and amp skids 6' x 3' on wheels) and limited on the second stage (sizes 8' x 8' x 1' and amp skids 6' x 3' on wheels).

BACKDROPS: There will be a truss at the rear of the stage from which we will fly your backdrop on the Main Stage (backdrops cannot be

Figure 301 Excerpt from artist information packs, advising of the time the band and their back line should be on site.

Changeover & Sound check

Sound checks are ONLY available to the headline artist, there will be time for a line check ONLY during your changeover.

Risers are on rotation, and we will endeavour to have at least 1 riser available to you 3 hours before your stage time, with any additional risers becoming available as soon as possible after this time.

Please advance your riser requirements carefully, as we might not be able to accommodate any changes on the day.

Please ensure you provide stage plans and channel lists in advance. Any artist failing to start promptly due to late arrival or being ill prepared will have the delay taken off their performance time. Please note there is a fine imposed by the local council should we overrun our curfew. Any artist contributing to an overrun will incur that penalty.

Figure 302 Another arrival time example

reason to park there!

ARRIVAL TIME

In order to facilitate the smooth, uninterrupted running of the show, please make sure your backline is on site and at the relevant stage **at least** four (4) hours before your allotted stage time. The artist needs to be onsite at least two (2) hours before your set time. This will give everyone enough time to get set up so that we are ready to go on time. Late arrival may affect your set up and the length of your set. **If you arrive too late to set up for your allotted stage time then you will not be playing – or indeed getting paid! So please be there.** If you are running late please contact the production office or the stage manager of your stage as early as you can so that at least we know where you are and what is going on.

VEHICLE PASSES

Figure 303 The message is clear: get on site at least 3 hours before you perform.

Collect Your Accreditation

You will need specific accreditation or 'passes' to drive onto the site, access the stage and dressing rooms, hospitality areas, etc. when you arrive at the festival. (see figure 304). Collecting your passes can become a drawn-out and bewildering task, especially stressful if you're running late.

Some festivals prefer sending out the passes to all the artists beforehand, addressing them to the tour manager, artist manager, or booking agent. This approach is convenient since you can arrive at the festival with your passes, eliminating the need to locate the 'artist accreditation hut' upon arrival. However, if you're touring during the summer, you might not be at home, in your office, or even in the country when the festival dispatches the passes. In such cases, you'll need to pick them up on site.

I highlight this because I've encountered some comical situations while trying to secure the right accreditation for my band and crew at certain festivals. The real headache is that you need a pass to get in, but you have to get in to pick up that pass! This often results in peculiar exchanges with security or stewards, explaining your need to enter the site to collect the passes you don't yet have, culminating in desperate pleas like "can you let me in, PLEASE?"

Different festivals have varied approaches to tackle this dilemma, with some more effective than others. You should therefore expect additional delays when planning your festival commute (refer to 'Get There On Time' above). Festivals are also vigilant about preventing the sneaking in of people, illegal substances, or other potential security threats. As such, security checks for every artist or crew vehicle are the norm. You might sneak your friend Dave in by hiding him behind the bass amp in your van, but festival organisers are wise to such tactics. They especially expect such antics from younger, novice bands, and DJs, and they strongly disapprove of any attempts to bring in extra friends or beer kegs. So, please refrain from such actions (see figure 305).

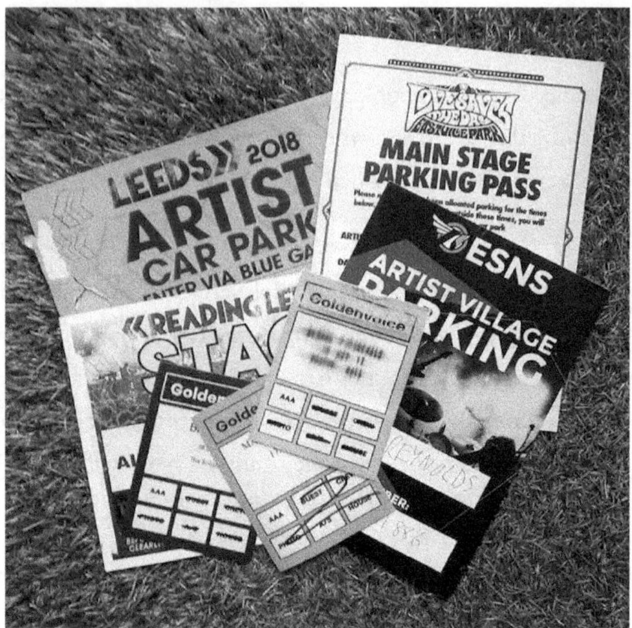

Figure 304: Artist and vehicle passes required to enter a festival.

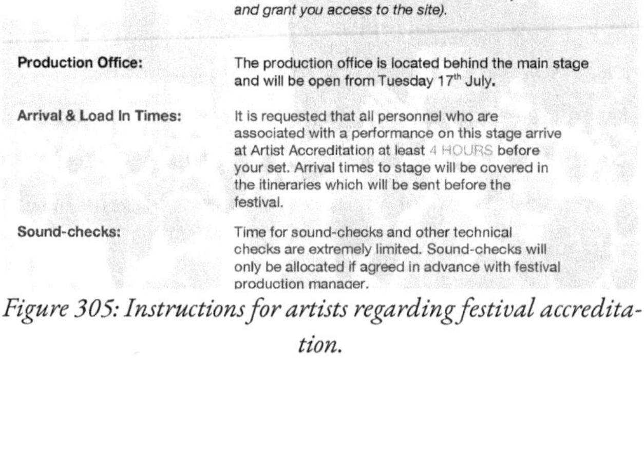

EVENT INFORMATION:

Artist Accreditation: Artist accreditation is located at the front desk of the Jodrell Bank's Discovery Centre, in front of the artist's parking area. The opening hours are 09:00- 00:00

(Any arrivals outside this time need be pre-arranged with elds.co.uk This will ensure that there is someone available to accredit your artists and grant you access to the site).

Production Office: The production office is located behind the main stage and will be open from Tuesday 17th July.

Arrival & Load In Times: It is requested that all personnel who are associated with a performance on this stage arrive at Artist Accreditation at least 4 HOURS before your set. Arrival times to stage will be covered in the itineraries which will be sent before the festival.

Sound-checks: Time for sound-checks and other technical checks are extremely limited. Sound-checks will only be allocated if agreed in advance with festival production manager.

Figure 305: Instructions for artists regarding festival accreditation.

Meet Your Host - the Artist Liaison Person

After arriving at a modern, outdoor, green-field festival, your 'band host', or 'artist liaison' person will greet you. These people fulfil the role of the representative for the promoter/organiser, and are there to welcome the music artists to the event, act as liaison between the artists and the stage manager, and attend to all dressing room, hospitality, and non-technical requests, issues and challenges that the artist may have.

Go Straight To The Stage

After you arrive on site and sort out the access for your band, crew, and vehicle, head straight to the stage where you'll perform. Meet the stage manager or the artist liaison person for that stage, and discuss load-in, changeover, and stage times. Though you might feel drawn to the backstage or 'artist VIP Village' area to mingle with other bands and artists, resist that urge. Sometimes, the artist liaison might even steer you directly to the dressing rooms, acting like you're just there to party and live it up. (Yep, that's a joke.)

Your priority should be to get your equipment-loaded vehicle to your performance stage. Determine whether your vehicle can stay there or if you must move it elsewhere. At some big festivals, like Glastonbury in the UK and Pukkelpop in Belgium, band vehicles can't access backstage areas. This means you'll unload your gear, transfer it to an official festival vehicle, and then drive it to the stage. This tiresome process is called cross-loading, and it's a pain, primarily because it takes up more of your precious time. For instance, look at the Glastonbury festival site map in Figure 306. Most artist vehicles, especially sleeper buses, have to stay at the Red Gate (north on the map). Now imagine the challenge of moving your gear to the Park Stage (south on the map).

Cross-loading gets more complicated since festivals often lack efficient methods to transport gear, bands, and crew to the stage. While they're eager to provide shuttle services, like EZ-Go buggies or John Deere 'Gator's (see Figure 307), for artists, they seem to forget the importance of getting everyone and everything to the actual performance area. If you think I'm exaggerating, remember I've seen this chaos for over 25 years. It's astonishing how some festivals struggle with the simple task of moving equipment, vehicles, the band, and the crew to the stage promptly.

So, the game plan: Once on site, get your vehicle and gear to the stage ASAP. Link up with the stage manager, discuss the details I mentioned earlier, and have your audio engineer chat with the stage audio crew to ensure they're up-to-date with your requirements. Once you've sorted all that, then you can head over to the plush 'artist village' and check out your backstage digs.

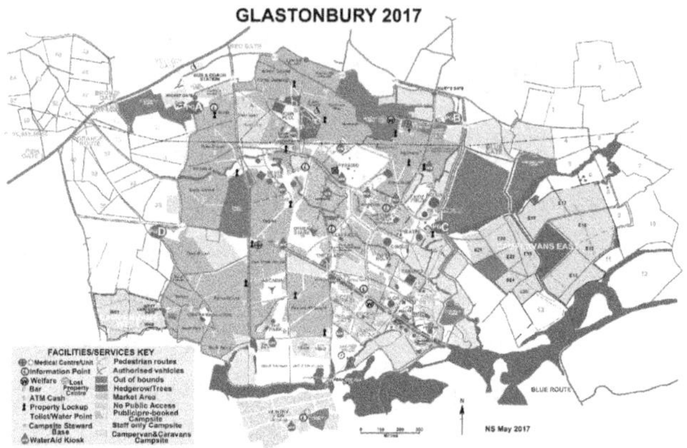

Figure 306: A map of the Glastonbury festival site. You can waste serious time trying to get across this site.

Figure 307: While EZ-GO buggies are great for moving people around festival sites, they're no good for cross-loading equipment from vans and trucks to the stage.

Take Everything You Need With You

Make sure that every member of your touring party has everything they need with them for the show when leaving the transport. This applies especially if you have to cross-load, or if the organisers direct you to park away from the stage where you are performing. Your vehicle is likely to be a considerable distance from your stage if this happens, and getting to it, and back again, could take a long time. In-ear monitor buds, vocal steamers, stage wear, USB memory drives, plectrums, and reeds are examples of items crucial to an artist's performance, and typical of the stuff that gets left in vehicles that are parked miles away.

Tell The Audience Who You Are

You read about the fact that "The Audience Is Not There to See You (Or Anyone Else)" in Part 2, and it's good to remember that when you are performing. The audience, who may wander by your stage/into your tent as you perform, needs to know who you are. So, tell them. Announce your name clearly over the mic at least three times in the set: once after the first couple of songs, once in the set's middle, and once before introducing the last song. Announcing your band name is important at festivals. Music artists might drop out, be late, get replaced, or even have their set times changed on different stages. The printed festival guides that are given out (or sold on entry) will, therefore, be incorrect, and even the mighty Clashfinder (Figure 308) can't keep up with every-minute change. So, don't leave it to chance - announce your name. You don't want the casual fan to discover you and yet not know who you are.

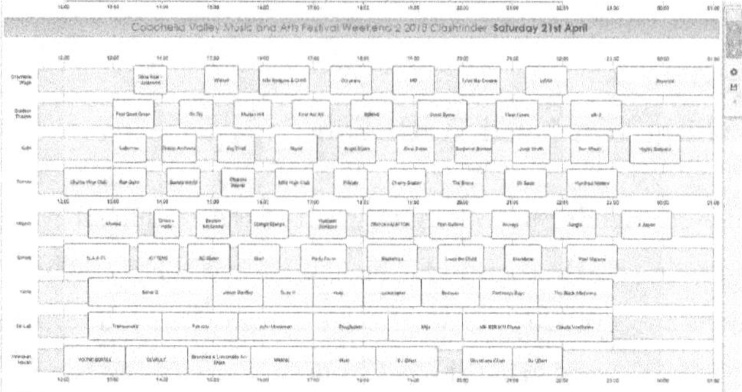

Figure 308: Clashfinder is essential for up-to-date line up and running order information at summer festivals. However, the information is user-generated and could be wrong, so let the audience know who you are, just in case.

Pros and Cons of Hanging a Backdrop

A backdrop is a great way to announce who you are. Any photos or shaky phone videos of your performance will display your backdrop, showcasing your name or logo for everyone to see (Figure 309). However, making a durable, road-worthy backdrop can be costly. If you're considering using one for your summer festival appearance, discuss it with the promoter during the advancing process. You can't simply show up at a festival expecting to hang your backdrop. Some festivals restrict backdrop usage to headline acts, and every venue, including festivals, will need assurance that your backdrop meets local and national fire safety regulations.

A suitable backdrop should be large enough for a festival stage, ranging from a flat-bed truck to a 70-foot wide 'orbit stage', but also functional for club and theatre shows. For instance, a 12' x 20' backdrop fits a festival stage nicely but is too large for most clubs or theatres. Ensure your backdrop has ties and hoops for attachment to fly-bars and uses fire-retardant materials. Also, ensure the manufacturer provides a certificate verifying the backdrop's flame-resistant quality.

Instead of a physical backdrop, consider high-quality video or image files for display on festival screens. Many electronic music festivals feature a 'video wall' as a stage backdrop, perfect for showcasing your name or logo. Organisers will provide details about the festival stage's video capabilities during the advance process (Figure 310). This guidance will include acceptable image file formats, with *.mov files typically being a good fit. You may need to consult a film, video, or photographic expert to craft a file with your name and logo. Once created, send this to the festival production team, similar to how you'd send your audio show files (refer to 'Show Files' in part two). I also suggest bringing a copy on a USB drive, just in case the on-site video team didn't receive your file.

Figure 309: A festival stage, showing an artist's own backdrop in position

Additional DJ equipment can be provided on request

Lighting

Control
Avolites - Tiger Touch 2 - Cat5 to Enttec datagate mk Artnet – 8 universes
5 x 5 pin dmx lines
1 x DMX buffer
3 x 100m Cat 5

Fixtures
12 x Robe - Pointies
8 x GLP X4 Moving wash
8 x Philips IP Estrip
4 x Martin Atomic 3000
4 x 2 cell Blinders
8 x RGBWA+UV 220watt 25Deg Par cans for stage wash.
1 x Jem ZR33 Smoke machine
1 x Barrel fan
1 x Smoke factory - Tour hazer

Venue Lighting
32 x 1m RGB LED rods LED
16 x RGBWA+UV 220watt 25Deg LED Pars cans
2 x Chauvet Geyser

Video

40 x V8 Outdoor LED Panel MK1 1000x500mm

2 x 100m Cat 5

LED screen Controller DVI input 1024 x 768@60Hz
Resolume Arena V6 server at FOH
1 x operator + screen tech

Figure 310: Information from a festival, included in the 'artist information' document, about the video screens or panels being supplied.

Don't Tell The Audience About Your New Songs

Please don't be one of those music acts who says "This is a new one," for any song in your set. To a new listener, all your songs are new. For well-known bands, announcing new material often prompts the audience to think, "I'll head to the bar, use the restroom, or see another band." Don't give potential fans a reason to leave.

Also, refrain from saying:

"We've just learnt this one." This implies a lack of rehearsal or preparedness, which disrespects the audience.

"We've never played this before." It suggests spontaneity, which can be good, and also suggests a poor rendition of the song. Not so good.

Commenting on the weather, like, "It's so hot/cold/windy up here." The audience wants entertainment, not reminders of their current environment.

"Is it loud enough?" or "How does it sound?" The FOH sound engineer might feel that you lack trust in them if you ask, "Is it loud enough?" or "How does it sound?".

Ensure everything you say keeps the audience engaged. Avoid reminding them they're in an outdoor setting, whether it's muddy or otherwise.

Streaming and Broadcast Rights

Continuing the thought that festival-goers are there to 'sample' or dive into a range of bands and music, it's clear that the whole festival experience matters to your fans. They're excited to see you on stage, but if they know your music, they might also want to dive into your whole festival day. This is especially true for fans who can't make it to the show. Sure, everyone can whip out their phone, film the show, and throw it on YouTube. But since that's become pretty common, it doesn't feel as special anymore. So, it's on you to capture and share those unforgettable moments from your debut summer festival performance. While sharing recorded smartphone clips is cool, think about taking it up a notch with live 'coverage' for your fans.

The live streaming of events, such as concerts, has become straightforward and cheap, thanks to platforms like Facebook Live, Twitch, YouTube Live streaming, and Instagram Stories. Streaming your performance might be the first thing that comes to mind, but there's stuff you need to think about. Promising a live stream might discourage some fans from coming to see you (though it's unlikely, given how fans like to 'sample' various acts). But more importantly, you might end up breaking some broadcasting rules set by the festival's contract with you (refer to Figure 311). Always double-check your contract to make sure you're allowed to record and stream your performance.

A better use of live streaming is showing off your backstage moments. That's a part of the festival that fans can't see, even if they're there. Sharing this can make the bond with your fans feel closer. How about a Q&A from your swanky backstage dressing room? Or maybe having someone tail you around the artist hospitality area while you mingle with other bands and road crew? These are exclusive moments most people won't experience unless they're watching your live stream.

Boost this band-fan connection further by crafting unique hashtags for your festival appearance. Stamp all your live content with it and get your fans to use the same hashtag for their posts. A smart way to design your hashtag might be to combine the official festival hashtag with your band's name, like #YourBandNameCoachella, and also using the official hashtag by itself.

production Information for further details.

12. Broadcast arrangements and press

The Festival's host broadcaster for 2014 is the British Broadcasting Corporation. The BBC is a public service broadcaster and Glastonbury 2014 will be broadcast by way of live television on four channels in the United Kingdom (BBC1, BBC2, BBC3 and BBC4); available by way of live or 'as live' internet streams on bbc.co.uk; On the so called red button (additional channels); available by way of extensive live radio coverage on the BBC's public service radio stations. Please note that BBC television broadcast are available on the BBC i-Player for 30 days post broadcast. It is a term of engagement for the Glastonbury Festival that artists performing on the Pyramid Stage, Other Stage, West Holts Stage, John Peel Stage and the Park Stage consent to the recording and broadcast of their performance (or an agreed part of their performance) for either live or 'as live' transmission by BBC Television and other services over the Festival Weekend in accordance with Schedule C attached hereto and that this recording as broadcast may be accessed using the 'red button' service over the Festival Weekend and by way of internet streaming for up to seven days in the following thirty days by way of the BBC i-Player. The BBC use standard form BBC-MU and where appropriate BBC-Equity talent engagement agreements which they will expect you and all performers with you to execute and receive payment under. The Festival will require the right to use up to four tracks for the Glastonbury 2014 international television highlights special for worldwide television distribution in all television formats and for worldwide radio distribution (including streamed radio) for a period of five (5) years from the date of the performance. You will procure that all performers including any session or backing musicians or other performers appearing on stage during your Performance will execute

Figure 311: An example of the broadcast rights and conditions that a festival may put in place. Please read this small print, so you don't get in trouble by 'broadcasting' something for which you don't have the rights.

Get Plenty of Assets

You might not livestream on the day. Many open-air, green-field festivals sits have very poor mobile phone coverage, and nonexistent Wi-Fi. That doesn't mean you shouldn't have your phones constantly recording or have someone videoing you. Plan to get plenty of assets even if you can live steam - you won't regret it when you are trying to fill your social media calendar with captivating video.

Register Your Performance with the Performing Rights Organisations

Besides earning money for your festival performance, you can get paid when someone performs your songs - if you register with a performing rights organisation (PRO). Organisations like ASCAP, BMI, SESAC, and PRS For Music are all PROs, and collect royalties for the public performance and broadcast of your compositions. Once you join a PRO, you can earn royalties from your live performances. In the UK, for example, the PRS collects for live performances at most venues, whether they're part of a tour. In the U.S., however, you'll only earn royalties from live performances if you're on one of the top 200 grossing tours, as listed by Pollstar magazine.

Royalties from performances get divided among all composers and songwriters. Festival organisers need a licence from the PRO to host live music and they pay a fee for that licence. The income from these fees then goes to the songwriters. For context, PRS For Music, the UK's main PRO, charges venues and promoters 5% of the total ticket sales. So, when Glastonbury Festival sold tickets worth £74 million in 2024, they probably paid around £3.5 million PRS For Music. PRS For Music would have distributed that £3.5 million to the relevant songwriters and composers.

It's crucial to connect with a PRO representative on the day of your performance and provide them with a list of songs you played, their composers, and your publishing company, if applicable. You'll often see PRO reps backstage gathering this information or encouraging unregistered artists to sign up. The forms they distribute can be a hassle to complete. That's why I always carry a pre-typed list of songs, composers, and publisher details for the band I represent when at festivals. I hand this over to the PRO rep. They appreciate it because it's clear, legible (thanks to being computer-generated), and they can easily input it into their system. Sometimes, I've even emailed the document directly to the PRO from my phone on the spot. Refer to Figure 312 for an example.

MILLIONS OF AMERICANS

	COMPOSER(S)	PUBLISHER
SCORE	Ben Green/ Dominic Hart/ Andy Ray	Sony ATV/ BMG Chrysalis Music/ Quincy Jones Music Publishing
LIVE POWER	Ben Green/Andy Ray	Sony ATV// Quincy Jones Music Publishing
VERSION FOUR	Ben Green/ Dominic Hart/ Andy Ray	Sony ATV/ BMG Chrysalis Music/ Quincy Jones Music Publishing.
ARM MYSELF	Ben Green/ Dominic Hart/ Andy Ray	Sony ATV/ BMG Chrysalis Music/ Quincy Jones Music Publishing
SOMETHING TO KNOW	Andy Ray	Quincy Jones Music Publishing
DESPAIR	Ben Green/ Dominic Hart/ Andy Ray	Sony ATV/ BMG Chrysalis Music/ Quincy Jones Music Publishing
RUNNING TO YOU	Ben Green/ Dominic Hart/ Andy Ray	Sony ATV/ BMG Chrysalis Music/ Quincy Jones Music Publishing
ENDLESS	Andy Ray	Quincy Jones Music Publishing
CAPITAL GAINS	Ben Green/ Dominic Hart/ Andy Ray	Sony ATV/ BMG Chrysalis Music/ Quincy Jones Music Publishing
MY USA	Ben Green/ Dominic Hart/ Andy Ray	Sony ATV/ BMG Chrysalis Music/ Quincy Jones Music Publishing
OVER AND OVER	Ben Green/ Andy Ray	BMG Chrysalis Music/ Quincy Jones Music Publishing
GAINING	Andy Ray	Quincy Jones Music Publishing
LAST TIME	Ben Green/ Dominic Hart/ Andy Ray	Sony ATV/ BMG Chrysalis Music/ Quincy Jones Music Publishing

Figure 312: My pre-typed song, composer, and publisher sheet that I email directly to the appropriate PRO after each festival performance.

You Will Sell No Merch at a Festival

"The lifeline of any touring band is merch (merchandise)" is a refrain commonly echoed online. But anyone who's manned a merch stall knows the struggle. Each sale is a hard-won battle, and the profits are slim. Earning from merch items like band t-shirts, hoodies, and stickers is as challenging as profiting from your music.

That's why I'm always taken aback when bands I work with brim with enthusiasm about festival merch sales, anticipating great earnings from a festival crowd. They reason that even if they sell to just 1% of a 3000-strong crowd, they'd make 30 sales.

But here's the reality: you won't make any sales from festival merch. And if I am wrong and you do make sales, the costs and time invested might wipe out your profits. Need proof? Here are reasons based on my experience:

1. Overwhelming Choice: Every band at a festival contributes a design to the festival T-shirt board, leading to decision paralysis for attendees (Figure 313). Most end up buying the official festival shirt, if they buy at all.

2. Stiff Competition: Festivals offer a plethora of non-band merchandise – food, beer, phone charging – all vying for attendees' money, leaving little for your t-shirt.

3. Visibility Issues: Third-party companies handle festival merch sales and typically display a sample from each band at merch booths. This works if you've partnered with a merch company like Bravado (see Figure 314), who can dispatch your items in advance. If not, you might deliver them on performance day, navigating through festival grounds to find the merch hub. With so many bands across multiple stages and days, your merch can get lost in the mix. If it's not visible, it won't sell.

4. Pricing Issues: The third-party merch company, in collaboration with headline acts, dictates the prices. Your band's shirts will cost the same as those of seasoned headliners, deterring new fans with steep prices.

5. Indifference: Many festival-goers are there to sample different genres and bands. They're unlikely to commit to one particular band's merch.

6. Festival Reluctance: Many festivals are steering clear of the merch hassle. The logistical demands, coupled with high commissions and zero sales, have led several to drop band merch sales.(Figure 315)

My advice? Skip the official festival merch stalls. If you want to try, announce a meet-up point from the stage and sell your merch there. (Just be cautious with cash on festival grounds.) You are better off paying the concession money towards hiring a videographer who will film you all day, thus generating lots of video assets.

Alternatively, spread the love: give away free items to the crowd, even if it strains your finances.

Figure 312: My pre-typed song, composer, and publisher sheet that I email directly to the appropriate PRO after each festival performance.

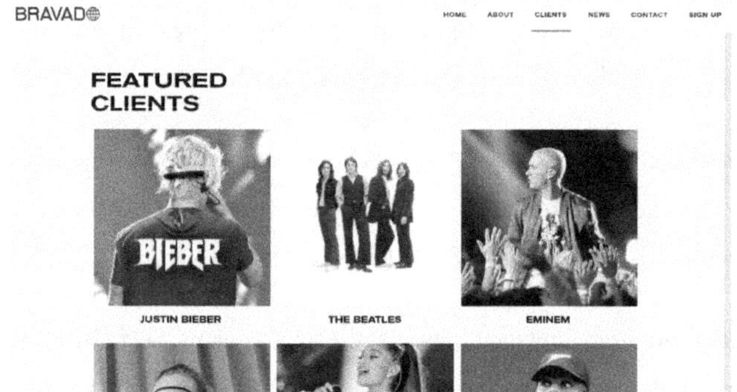

Figure 314: Bravado, a music merch specialist, can manage your tour or festival merch sales, though they'll take commission of sales.

Please note that we do not to do merchandise at SGP – bands are welcome to try and sell merch themselves at the stage, but we will not be offering a place to sell. The reason being is that even our headliners have only ever sold 1 t-shirt max. Our audience is not the kind that buys merchandise, even our festival programme is given away free at the pedestrian gate.

Figure 315: Secret Garden Party in the UK is among the festivals that no longer sell music artist merch.

Checklist and Conclusion

You now have the information you need to make the most of your festival performance - and you will become an old hand, appearing at green-field, open-air festivals across Europe and the US for many years to come.

Remember, playing any gig is primarily about giving existing fans what they want, and trying to appeal to people to become new fans. That involves 'playing the hits' or performing a fantastic show. Both can be difficult within the constraints of modern music festivals - no sound check, short changeovers, too many choices for the audience and sound level limits all conspire to create less-than-perfect conditions in which to shine.

However, you have now read all I know about the various issues and challenges involved in festival appearances. You should be able to expect and react accordingly. Just in case, I will leave you with a checklist you should follow to play your first open-air music festival to the best of your ability.

Checklist

The following is a brief list of the main activities and concerns you should have when approaching your first open-air, green-field, music performance.

1. Decide who will be in charge of all this.

It's a lot of work, and it's a lot simpler when one person does it all. Trust me on this.

2. Book your transport and hotels.

Do both now.

3. Make a proper input list and stage plan.

Find someone to construct one for you if you don't know how/are unsure/cannot be bothered. Your live sound engineer or local PA rental company will help you with this. Make sure you specify stage positions on the stage plan and don't swap places on the day of the performance!

4. Treat the advance process seriously.

Read everything you receive from the festival organisers, and if you receive nothing (or not much) ask them for it. The advance process is to help them, as much as you, and the festival people need to know everything about you and your technical requirements. At the least you need to know how long your set time is, what time is changeover, and what time you are on stage.

5. Find out if the festival can supply rolling risers.

You might not need them, and if you do, ask about the quantity and availability of any risers the festival can supply.

6. Sort out you set list.

You know the time you have for your performance from the advance, so now figure out how many songs you can play in that time and what order they should go in. Then create and print a version of your set list to give or email to your PRO - complete with composers names and publisher details.

7. Sort out your guest list.

Tastemakers and those who deserve a big 'thank-you' only.

8. Make sure you know where you are going, and how long it will take to get there.

Google Maps may say it's 2 hours from your house to the festival site. It also takes a long time to get onto a large site, such as Glastonbury or Coachella, and you will compete for road space with the thousands of people who are also travelling to the festival. Take all this into account when planning your journey.

9. Record lots of video and audio assets

Keep the smartphones running, especially when you are in the areas the fans dont see. The video and audio assets you acquire will be social media gold for the rest of the year.

10. Remind yourself to enjoy the whole thing!

About the author

Andy Reynolds has worked as an international concert tour manager and audio engineer for over 30 years. He has toured continuously during this time, working on an average of 200 shows per year. Andy has worked for such artists including Maribou State, The Pierces, Maverick Sabre, All-American Rejects, House of Pain, Machine Head, Nightmares On Wax, Pavement, Roots Manuva, Super Furry Animals, Utah Saints, Skunk Anansie, and Squarepusher, as well as tours with U2, Whitney Houston, Manic Street Preachers, and Foo Fighters. His touring experience encompasses stadiums, arenas, theatres, pubs, bars, clubs, outdoor festivals, rooftops, subway stations, cruise ships, mountainsides, and muddy fields.Andy is also the author of '***The Live Music Business: Management and Production of Concerts and Festivals, Third Edition***' a comprehensive guide for students and the curious.

Learn more about Andy at www.livemusicbusiness.com

Please leave a review

I hope you enjoyed this book and found it useful. I also hope you will want to leave a review on Barnes & Noble, Nook, Apple Books, Amazon, or wherever you buy your books. Your support and opinion matters to me, and it makes a difference to everything I do. A review will also tell other readers what you didn't, or did, like about this mini-guide.

Thanks again for reading.

Andy

www.ingramcontent.com/pod-product-compliance
Lightning Source LLC
LaVergne TN
LVHW010503160826
845677LV00012B/2633